# Lithic Scatter
*and Other Poems*

Other Works by Karla Linn Merrifield

—Poetry—

*Attaining Canopy: Amazon Poems*

*The Ice Decides: Poems of Antarctica*

*Liberty's Vigil, The Occupy Anthology: 99 Poets among the 99%*
(co-edited with Dwain Wilder)

*The Urn*

*The Etowah River Psalms*

THE DIRE ELEGIES: 59 Poets on Endangered Species of North America
(co-edited with Roger M. Weir)

*Dawn of Migration and Other Audubon Dreams*

*Godwit: Poems of Canada*

*Midst*

—Photography—

*The Green Bookcase* (with essay by William Heyen)

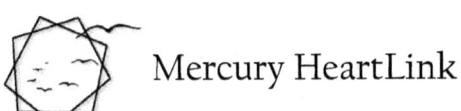

## More Praise for *Lithic Scatter and Other Poems*

No tourist guide to badlands, canyonlands, desert monuments, *Lithic Scatter* is a passionate, precise field record of knowledge won through bruising encounters with rockface, rapids, scorching sands. Won too from patient encounters with Anasazi artifacts, O'Keeffe paintings, *outpost country, exile country, / loneliest dust-and-stone country that defies the grid / of your imagination*. Somehow, in this masterful collection, the author has been able to fuse the dithyrambic to the scientific, to present us the rough specimen alongside the river-polished stone. Far from a bruising read, *Lithic Scatter* is a *Wunderkabinett* of earthly delights.
—John Roche, author of *The Joe Poems: the Continuing Saga of Joe the Poet*

In this fine collection, the first poem, "Dancing with Green Bees," sets the joyous tone as Karla Linn Merrifield, a widely traveled poet, revels in the landscape and celebrates the wisdom and lives of our native inhabitants. From ephemeral bees to ancient stones, nothing is beyond her eager examination; indeed, a tiny cobble will set her on a flight of wonderment and philosophical conjecture. Stylistically, this book is a marvel of musical lines, such as when she describes "arriving like snowmelt in spring from the slickrock flanks of the Chuska Mountains." Color is also a constant revelation: a black bear is "in a cinnamon morning coat" and "bald domes wake from violet sleep." The book has its somber moments, especially when Merrifield confronts the destructive nature of modern man; touches of wry humor, too, such as in the poem where she contrasts dragonflies with helicopters ("draconian Homeland Security spawn.") *Lithic Scatter and Other Poems* will strengthen Merrifield's considerable reputation as an American naturalist-poet.
—Laury A. Egan, author of *Beneath the Lion's Paw* and *Snow, Shadows, a Stranger*

In *Lithic Scatter*, poet-guardian of the Earth Karla Linn Merrifield tosses stones in the ten directions and asks us to find the treasures that lie beneath the surface they land upon. She tells us "Landscape bids you to absorb time." We best listen to what her landscapes reveal because written beneath their "parched, rough skin folded and folded over bones" lie histories – history of where we came from, histories of who we are. What are these bones, and what do they implore us to do? Having walked, paddled, scrambled on hands and knees through brush and gravel wash, and having sat with the Earth for decades, Merrifield knows – "even stones utter mythic stories…They wrap me in their receptive skin to listen and in turn receive." So take this beautiful book of poems forged in the crucible of Western landscapes, find a favorite piece of geology, sit, read a few poems, listen to what frog, raven, bison and painter have to say about time, because in the West "time is different" and Merrifield's poem-maps show the way.
—Michael G. Smith, poet and chemist; Jentel and Andrews Experimental Forest Artist-in-Residence

In *Lithic Scatter and Other Poems*, Karla Linn Merrifield immerses herself in the energy of the natural world, then takes us on a journey of the American West through eyes attuned to that energy. With her we travel as mystics, learn things we would not otherwise know—how quartz sparkles in the San Juan River above the Colorado, how a mountain stream lives its course to a canyon river, how prehistoric women exist near the mouths of ancient caves. Because Merrifield grows into these landscapes and allows them to grow into her, we experience their magic as she does, in moments of powerful peace and ecstatic union: "I fly over/ carved clay mesas, spires, canyons,/ a shadow upon shadows bringing/ another thunderstorm, needed rain,/ floating on a good tailwind." Such sharing strengthens our humanity, reminds us of the need to attend to both ourselves and Earth.
—Colleen Powderly, author of *Split*

# Lithic Scatter
*and Other Poems*

Karla Linn Merrifield

Lithic Scatter and Other Poems
Copyright ©2013 Karla Linn Merrifield

ISBN: 978-0-9882279-9-6
Publisher: Mercury HeartLink
Printed in the United States of America

Inside and back cover author photos by Roger M. Weir
Cover photo, "Self-Portrait, c. 1140 CE," by Karla Linn Merrifield
Interior photos, "Front-Page News," "Stone Shaman" and "Petroglyph TV" by Karla Linn Merrifield

All rights reserved. This book, or sections of this book, may not be reproduced or transmitted in any form without permission from the author.

Permission is granted to educators to create copies of individual poems for classroom or workshop assignments.

Mercury HeartLink
www.heartlink.com
editor@heartlink.com

# Contents

Finding Stanzas in the Stone     xix

## I.

| | |
|---|---|
| Dancing with Green Bees | 3 |
| Feet of Clay | 4 |
| Badlands Beauty | 6 |
| Parsing Mato Paha | 7 |
| Badlands Sutra | 8 |
| Rainier Trail Guide | 9 |
| Everything's Talking | 10 |
| Wooden Stone | 11 |
| High-Altitude Spectrum | 12 |
| Making Beds | 14 |
| Summer Morning in Muir's Park | 15 |
| Magnitude 5.4 | 16 |

## II.

| | |
|---|---|
| Amid the Bighorns | 21 |
| Historical Marker, State Route 158 | 22 |
| Cody Museum I – Taxidermy | 24 |
| Cody Museum II – Preservation | 25 |
| Raven Woman's Artifact, 1862 | 26 |

|  |  |
|---|---|
| At "VV 74 Fate Bell" Archeological Site | 27 |
| Caution: Women at Work | 29 |
| Copters | 30 |

# III.

|  |  |
|---|---|
| Rocky Mountain Lows | 35 |

## Dancing: Durango and Silverton Narrow Gauge Suite

|  |  |
|---|---|
| I. Animas River | 36 |
| II. 12° | 37 |
| III. Motions | 38 |
| IV. Wild Westing | 39 |
| V. Into Durango | 40 |

## Walkabout Rivers

|  |  |
|---|---|
| I. THE COLORADO | 41 |
| Mile 0: For Starters | 41 |
| Mile 75.5: SOS | 42 |
| Mile 166: Canyon Colors | 43 |
| Mile 213.5: Stranded | 44 |
| II. THE SAN JUAN | 45 |
| Entering the San Juan below Montezuma Creek | 45 |

Anthropology 101: Beneath No-Name Ruins — 46
Flow Going above Comb Ridge — 47
Shall We Gather at the River? — 48
Approaching 0 Flow CFS — 49
One Hard Lesson — 50
Top to Bottom — 52
Marie's Corn Rosary — 53

## A Vocabulary of Circular Forms

At the Ranch above Taos — 54
   I. David Herbert Lawrence
   II. Georgia O'Keeffe
   III. Karla Linn Merrifield
Georgia O'K — 56
O'Keeffe: "Circling Around Abstraction" — 57
From KLM to GO'K: Santa Fe Watercolor
   Abstraction on Paper: Juniper, Titmouse — 58
The Talisman Artifact — 59
Painting of Sagebrush (Green), Clouds (White),
   And Raven (Black) on Rice Paper with Wax — 60
Land Marking — 61
The Void — 62
A Fragile Defiance — 63
It Is You Who Are Essential — 64
Mesa Verde Vision — 65

| | |
|---|---|
| Under the Sleeping Rainbow | 66 |
| The Missing Force at 36° N Latitude, 107° 57' 30" Longitude | 68 |
| Be Now My Anasazi | 70 |
| Amazons of the Anasazi Follow the Chimney Rock Tour Guide | 71 |
| *Araneidae* Among the Anasazi | 74 |
| Stations of the Rock | 76 |
| Throb | 78 |
| Lithic Scatter | 79 |

## Acknowledgments 83

## About the Author 87

# Lithic Scatter
*and Other Poems*

*For Andy Hutchinson, Kate Thompson,
Chuck and Amy Wales, R. J. Johnson, and Brad Dimock
of the dories*

*In memoriam,
Derald Stewart, Zen boatman*

*for Nick Bartlett, Georgia Garr and Nicholas Bartlett
of the* Tahoma

*and for Roger,
ever my magpie muse*

*The size of the place that one becomes
a member of is limited only by
the size of one's heart.*
—Gary Snyder, *Back on the Fire: Essays*

# Finding Stanzas in the Stone

Primal time, not prime time. Geologic time, not Timex minutes. Sacred time, not Daylight Savings Time. Positively Dreamtime, I tell you.

Like most modern *Homo sapiens sapiens*, I seek time off from the quotidian, and am lucky enough to get it. Often. Several times I've found it, for example, among the ghosts of the ancient Anasazi at Canyon de Chelly National Monument, sacred *Diné* (Navajo) country, in Arizona. There I've made pilgrimages deep into the canyon to monumental Spider Rock because the rock is home to Spider Woman, whom the *Diné* say taught women to weave. I return hoping maybe she will teach *me* to weave – in words.

I go to be amid rock that's 280-million-years-old, where traces of human life remain after more than 2000 years. But in my version of escape to places like de Chelly, to prevent being further lithified by habit, I don't leave "work" behind. I go on an archeological expedition of sorts. I pick up a symbolic trowel and dig. It's the work of poetry I will do.

Spider Woman has taught me no poem can come until *I* come of age. Again. At 50 or 55 or 60. I must uncover my inner story at every age. I must chisel through the bedrock of my gregarious self to my quiet self, just as other poets and writers have done.

I follow archaic footsteps, a white woman – *biligana* (and a Yankee, no less). I scrape through my life's metaphoric layers to find the message that Spider Rock or Chimney Rock or Badlands rock or the rock of the Sierra Mountains, the rock of Mount Rainier always delivers to me when I place my hand on sandstone or granite, Vishnu schist or gneiss.

My first task? Sift out the tourist! She who on her first visit to de Chelly seventeen years ago bought a chunk of petrified wood as a souvenir from a shawled Navajo elder at an overlook. Was that me? 'Twas. But I've since learned that's no way to make a poem. And, should I lose track of that in the hot dusty swirls, I have a reminder from Navajo poet Laura Tohe who once e-mailed: "The tourist visits a place on a more superficial level....A poet leads you to an internal place." So, the carved jasper turtle I bought during my last visit from a young Navajo woman didn't reveal any secrets. Her words did, though: "Turtle means abundance, long life." And I said to myself, "Now, I'm getting somewhere." The rock speaks to its messengers and in turn Tohe and that stone-faced girl in her University of Arizona sweatshirt speak to me.

That same day, I make my way upcanyon in an old Army truck with guide and driver Ron Yazzie. We stopped to drop off a sack lunch for the diminutive shepherdess Maria Jake, sitting stoically in the shade of coyote willows, tending her sheep and goats. She'd been there since early morning, having made her way down a steep stony trail from the rim 1,000 feet above and she'd be there until dusk when she retraced her precarious path home. When I ask her age, Ron says simply, "She's 87."

***

In the process of weaving words, next comes the patient unearthing of a second, deeper layer. Aha! Essential stillness! I knew I could find it. Such a place is, after all, where "stillness matures," according to poet Catherine Savage Brosman. It does. The elemental afternoon summer sun sheds silent light on what I'd forgotten since my last trip to desert floor and rimrock. I'd traveled 2,000 miles there because, like Tohe, the canyon rocks speak directly to me: *Hágo, hágo* – come here, come here. Then, the canyon whispers, "Hush! Hush!" So I silence the words scurrying in my brain like pocket gophers to hear the rocks' red stony message.

Finally, I arrive at the base of Spider Woman, that 800-foot twin monolith, *Tse Na-asshjee-ii*. In moments such as these, I reach my final stage of excavation, I wield a fine brush to expose the outlines of my innermost being. In the hot June glare, looking up, up, craning my neck, I realize: I'm so very tiny at 5 feet, 4 inches. I'm also quite young – but a girl in comparison. Welcome to Dreamtime, girl.

***

And so it happens, just as Western writer Michael Engelhard claims it does: "We can only find nature's poetry when we perceive our own insignificance."

There, and throughout the American West, I find the lithic scatter that's been buried so long; I find the artifact of my true Self. I find the poem.

—KLM
January 2013

I.

## Dancing with Green Bees

Find your way to the third hearth
to become a woman of clay—again.

Just when you believe you are
the definition of thirst,
have endured too many erasures
sealed inside a sere landscape,
you will whirl into the dance
of dragonflies.

Or the dance of the green bees
—starting in the yellow sheen of morning,
of cactus bloom, of meadowlark, of the shining—
will fling you maiden-like beneath birdshadow.

The path to the third hearth
is strewn with surprises of sparkling quartzite.
You are amidst a fortress of rock, a cathedral of stone,
and the elemental particulate that has undergone
its many metamorphoses as you have.
Landscape bids you to absorb time,
breathe earth dust, the primordial.

There at the third hearth
the women of clay await you.
By their painted faces you will know them.

## FEET OF CLAY
*with lines from a Mexican folk song*

*Friend, when I am dead,*
*make a cup of the clay I become.*
                Day of rain in the Badlands:
                my feet sunk in gray clay
                that sucked at my sandals;
                water seeped in to fill footprints
                left by my rippled soles.

*And, if you remember me,*
*drink from it.*
                Some time later sun
                dried those imprints,
                but before the remaining rain
                drained away, a magpie alit,
                dropped its head, and drank.

*Should your lips cling*
*to the cup...*
                A mountain bluebird, piñon jay,
                and raven flew in for the last few drops
                on a scorching afternoon, and with wet throats,
                warbled, shrieked, cawed.
                Echoes rang off painted rocks until dusk.

*it will be my
earthly kiss.*

                Now, after dark, I fly over
                carved clay mesas, spires, canyons,
                a shadow upon shadows bringing
                another thunderstorm, needed rain,
                floating on a good tailwind.

## Badlands Beauty

She shows herself to me
for the first time—
full-faced, brazenly as crone,
Woman-Grown-Old,
each crenellation of age
worn unabashedly.
I feel the parched, rough skin
folded and folded over bones beneath.
When she does not shrink
from my stare, I draw closer,
listen to Her story told in dust
and learn that someday
I am to become
as beautiful as She.
I will slowly, slowly,
ever so slowly follow
her path toward fossils.

## Parsing Mato Paha

Under my skin is a nation of beings
and their cacophony of alien languages,
some particularly strange
—black-backed woodpecker, upland sandpiper;
some distantly familiar
—bobolink, gray jay.
Beneath ponderosa pine needles and
the silver-green berries of junipers
echo the voices of sun and wind.
Even stones metamorphic, igneous, sedimentary—
all the Earth's more enduring creatures—
utter their mythic stories into the night.
They wrap me in their receptive skin
to listen and in turn receive.

Note: Mata Paha *is the Lakota name for the Badlands*

## Badlands Sutra
### *with lines from Cid Corman's "The Tortoise"*

Geology is
terrible slowness,
overtaking haste.

There are things to be said.
No doubt.
But clay is silent.

To whom tell the silences?
The bison,
the bison.

Then there was a bird!
Some say warbler,
some say raven.

To go back,
to correct an error,
study the oxbow.

The land remains
desolate.
Let sandstone claim you.

The sky is empty.
Watch! Wait!
Prairie imparts patience!


*for John Heiser*

# Rainier Trail Guide

When frog spoke
her instructions began
plant your feet
on the earth

First peer downward
at the many
fungi and lichens
This is modesty

Now tilt upward
toward the canopy
of ancient treetops
This is majesty

Finally stare inward
Behold your fir
with its mosses
One another one

This is maternity
This is maturity

## Everything's Talking

Clouds are its language,
with wind verbs, river nouns.
Each Douglas fir punctuates
in two-hundred-foot exclamation points;
commas of cones strewn from on high
give this mountain's passenger pause.
Red alders in their silver skin speak
in a related tongue of green.
Out walking quietly, I translate
many slowly voiced, ephemeral words
into a message of hiddenness.
I will take another thousand years
to comprehend these meanings
just being formed in the evening,
in the cloud language of Mt. Rainier.

## Wooden Stone

Yes, my beloved child,
your mother was a tree,
one of the ancient ginkgo people,
and your father was a rock,
one of the old gneiss tribe.

Yes, my beloved child,
you were born of substances primordial,
creature of green and brown and gray,
once a seed, once a lava flow.

Yes, my beloved child,
I am your blessed midwife who now
witnesses another rebirth,
rising up from Columbia River shores
in the shadow of petroglyphs—
artists' notations of an unknown nation.

My beloved child, you became petrified
in glacial ridges, in volcanic fire,
made of the Mother and the Father,
and with my hands delivered
into cool forests, cold stone,
where you, my beloved child,
rest again in solid, quiet dignity
after ten thousand years of hidden longing.

## High-Altitude Spectrum

Black bear in cinnamon morning coat,
snoozing on a hefty snag, Ursus widespread,
more sequoia red than the trees at this hour.

Stellar's jays, giants themselves
among such corvids, more black
than iconic indigo and blue,

sassing the ravens in their shade,
the black birds' sharp calls sounding
raucous orange, more orange

than sunrise on bare granite.
Bald domes wake from violet sleep
and begin to glow.

Yellow-bellied marmots, more gold
than noon, rodentia auric,
perch on stony thrones.

Snowmelt has turned to white water;
the river's emerald pools and turquoise
eddies flash silver this mid-day

and all that is green—
lodgepole, sweat pine, Douglas fir,
all lichen, starburst and rock-posy alike—

shimmers a rainbow as if
a sudden summer thunderstorm
had washed the mountains iridescent.

And you, the witness of this Range of Light
that is the Sierra Nevada, see Her majesty
in living colors.

Tomorrow: wildflowers,
more avians,
and the wind.

## Making Beds

In an Intertidal Shellfish Enhancement Project
they plant geoducks and oysters to increase
harvest opportunities, warning me to avoid digging in areas
marked by red posts, to avoid immature bivalves.
I wonder what the clams say about Sequim Bay's program
and if black brants and white-winged scoters
obey the Department of Fish and Wildlife Service notices,
or pay the moorage fees— what it costs to float
above beds breeding the succulence and sweetness
of briny water the birds call home.

As I climb up above protected waters, I believe
in purer places, ones with no signs of what's being lost,
with no human intervention, no prescribed seasons,
no other hand controlling, no greed and creeping demand.
I come along too late for all but an aftertaste.
My mouth is dry; I swallow the prolific emptiness.

# Summer Morning in Muir's Park

In Half Dome's sharp shadow, monarch grips with dainty feet one pendulous milkweed bloom of thousands in many generous alpine meadows in this singular valley floor. But the rock-climber inching upward a half mile on El Capitan's vertical face sees only granite, curses its polish, oblivious to the glacier whose ghost is sheen on stone. Nor does the hang-glider, launching from the rim of Glacier Point to ride thermals, see her. Nor has he an eye for the golden eagle as she drifts downward that half mile, more.

These are Yosemite's daredevils today, three among all sierra risk-taking creatures: two thrill-seekers, men, toying with gravity while the glaciers melt; and a butterfly plying—with a numinous sense of mountains and glaciers— the petals of her benefactress for survival. She descends, lays her eggs, ascends, sips again, and flies two thousand miles, more.

# MAGNITUDE 5.4

This is the fault line:
five words
where I falter
and fall
into the Mojave Desert
of thoughtlessness.
One misstep, one slip.
Canyon floor brings me
to a halt, sharp-stoned
and searing, to the lip
of the boneyard.
Monzogranitic gravel grinds
into knees and palms;
its dun-colored, coarse graters
bloody the edge of my imagination.
I am face down,
spitting dust, spooked
by stone's empty eyes,
non compos mentis.
The San Andreas shifts.
The Earth underfoot comes
alive; it quakes
with enough desire for my flesh
to kill me.

II.

## Amid the Bighorns

snow swale

fog drift

stream rush

raven glide

If I am not crushed
by cliff slide
I will become
the summit

# Historical Marker, State Route 158

With beaded black eyes the vigilant white
sea gulls of Raritan Bay have glanced eastward

toward islands in the distance across
from Sandy Hook: Manhattan, Long, Fire, Ellis.

Tilting on lofty swoops, the birds remember
from their ancestors the generations of arrivals,

all those black-clothed Old World Jews in fetid holds,
pogrom-humbled once, now deep in steerage,

speaking Yiddish, mumbling diaspora Hebrew prayers,
until tossed ashore past the white surf, relieved of anguish.

But no Jersey *Larus delawarensis* ever learned
where that one surviving boatload finally landed,

one *shul* of sixty Russian immigrants, later
seeded near an unimaginable line, the $100^{th}$ Meridian.

No coastal avian could see that far—
the long Conestoga trails to a dozen sections, dozen families—

homesteaders in 1887—with their Torah,
undamaged by the voyage, safe at last

in a sod house on one-hundred-sixty acres,
in the blank ark of the sere open prairie.

*This place shall be named Beersheba,*
*and within months one of us shall marry,*
*one of us die, one of us be born;*
*so be the mitzvahs of Kansas.*

## Cody Museum I – Taxidermy

Two buffalo, stuffed and mounted:
one, poised to bellow, is perfectly
silent now, museum light in his glass eyes.
Can his spirit dream the prairie alive again?
Dream its wild, wild miles of grass, mud,
flies, fleas for thirty million of his species?

Or does he only see hunters
who took his tongue, leaving few tongues today
to speak buffalo and chant the vast meadow
of America into renewed green being.
Oh, great horned brown beasts,
*Tatanka*, long after your thundering centuries
have elapsed, all the museum's plundered ones sleep,
reflecting the West's shadowy history read
at a glance in a glass eyeball.

# Cody Museum II – Preservation

During the dark of the moon,
when the museum has shut
its doors for the night,
the seven silent birds
of Red Medicine Blanket wake.
This is medicine.

Redwing blackbird stirs first;
next kingfisher flutters.
Then wren, magpie, swallow,
killdeer, and sparrow voice
their release from the glass cage.
This is medicine.

No display case can restrain
them. Through the pane they pull
the wool behind their tails.
No alarm rings, no one sees
walls dissolve, gates evaporate.
This is medicine.

Red Medicine Blanket flies
and twirls toward a tipi,
to a shaman, to perform
a midnight rite chanted and danced
with feathers flying home.
This is medicine.

# Raven Woman's Artifact, 1862

The Tobacco Society blanket
asks for nothing
from the wind.
My medicine blanket
that I have lived to use again.
My blanket is a museum piece.
But it flies like a weather dancer
on wings of piñon jays pinned
to a red wool sky.
It hovers over the Universe
from beyond its glass display,
as the nighthawk stitched
onto a coarse red heaven did
once above Absaroka Mountain rivers.
One red-wing blackbird shed its scarlet blood
to dwell in the swirling world
of my red, red medicine blanket.

As with earth, as with rain,
this blanket of deer hide and trade beads
dreams through feathered time: our healing.

# At "VV 74 Fate Bell" Archeological Site

Willingly, in thirst,
I step through
your red portal.

Here is the only
way, one you had
painted with iron

oxide, bone marrow
and sotol on a limestone
wall beneath a broad

canopy streaked black
with manganese. Such
is the tenacious strength

of your art that
Cretaceous-era rock
parts, canyon enfolds

my body. I succumb.
O my Hunter,
I am your Gatherer

come to decipher
the ochre thread
of your story line

one-hundred-eighty
human generations
later, in a fiery flicker

of shamanic time.
For here, this now,
I am Pecos River Woman,

a trace of yellow
yucca twine, who
binds herself slowly

to your sacred staff.
Willingly, in hunger,
I receive, retrieve

seeds of your enchanted
genius, and from my entrancement
within your ancient

stone, thus return—
to my people,
full of your wild mind.

From the living side
I then sing of your vivid
petroglyphs so all may

remember you, remember our
brief prehistory, and this:
young love's arrival.

# Caution: Women at Work

They are in my fingertips yet, those
Archaic women of Seminole Canyon.
As they pounded sotol bulbs into flour
on a smooth flat boulder oiled to a patina
enduring eight thousand years, the mothers'
earnest breath seeped deeply
into pores of my hand. I caressed
the sandstone surface, of what in my age
would be a Formica countertop, also waist high.
So, yes, they are still in my wrists
and forearms, my shoulders respond with
an ache from the vibrations of their exertions.

Can't you hear the ancient brown women
of Seminole Canyon, their mashing, smashing
against strong rocks at cavern's edge?
And their gossip? Two sisters laboring
over paddles of juicy prickly pear cactus,
arguing whose husband is the better pictograph artist?
Whose creations, three-hundred-twenty generations later,
will draw tourists from distant regions
to stare and gasp at enduring shamanistic figures?
I stand among those travelers transfixed
by an afterimage of what we now disparage
as women's work, theirs and mine, ours.

## Copters

On the day when three subtropical dragonfly species
appeared at Galveston Island Beach, metallic imitations
patrol far overhead— the Coast Guard's
draconian Homeland Security spawn.

Gallardia daisies stalk sunflowers on young dunes,
blooming open to the menace above,
some going to seed; they heed not the spying beasts.
Laughing gulls maniacally cackle,
idling away hours along the wrack line.
From a loose rope strung low across the Gulf,
pelicans plunge one by one out of formation
into shallow waters, feeding according to
perfected instinct, ignoring the armed monsters.

Only *Homo sapiens* of the tourist variety,
myself included, lying on the sand are terrorized,
knowing those hovering creatures,
like practiced predators, take their prey alive.

III.

## Rocky Mountain Lows

Up another two thousand feet—
                                           and thirty
miles away—
                     there are mists blotting out details
of peaks,
          glacier-smothering,
                       white-snow eating,
swirling mists turning almost instantly to ice.
Mine are brooding isolated clouds
                     in a dozen rumpled gray tones,
swiftly fleeing,
             shaped for a storm.
If I cannot feel the bite,
             I can imagine it:
                         fanged,
relentless as the wind
                     and the force of gravity.
The gentleness you breathe off the east coast—
a classic lingering brand of still,
                 tame moisture,
cuts off your view, just as these indifferent mountains,
these bloodied Sangre de Cristos,
             do mine.
                   But down here
on the valley floor I am in the desert.

# Dancing: Durango and Silverton Narrow Gauge Suite

## I. Animas River

Oh, to be a mountain stream
sluicing down, down narrow clefts,
gushing over ledges, rushing on,
on with a roar between valley walls,
or whispering in high meadows
in myriad shades of green, silver;
froth and spume of whiteness,
moving over sandbars, moraine,
then granite and traces of ore;
yellow birches, balsam fir, beeches
stand by for this is where bears drink,
beavers build, and brook trout echo
the watermist rainbows
of a June afternoon.

Oh, what it must be to be me
when I begin to sing!

## II. 12°

Curved energy swelled up
from canyon floor to harness sun by day,
moonlight after dark.
Along its path that wild force invaded
roots of trees, plant and gourd seedlings
waiting for its arrival.
It swirled into and around the kivas,
at home in a circle of centeredness,
welcome at the round fire pit.
It curled over the bellies of wives
large with coming life and laureled
the heads of all those sitting in
silent private reverence
as it arced over their place on earth
and leapt to the sky on a rainbow
where the people saw its promise.
It continues its immense journey,
resounding in the cliffs at Mesa Verde,
remembering the ancient ones now seeking
the new ones: latter-day shamans
and poets and lovers holding their breath
as they dream.

## III. Motions

Young aspen leaves
when the wind rolls
down the canyon
Pine Needle Creek foaming
over and over boulders
on its way out
of the mountains
and hummingbirds feeding
on columbines at water's edge
in the evening
toward the end of spring
no stopping such wildness
until the heat of August
or until I forget

## IV. Wild Westing

Mid-stream black boulder
bears brunt of water rushing—
it shines its brightest.

Moose in the meadow:
two males dozing in dusklight,
but the cow watches.

Still Navajo sleep
all winter long in hogans—
I hear them snoring.

Spiders' webs catch dreams
to hold in dew drops at dawn.
They capture me, too.

At tree line, firs lean
slender green tips toward the crest.
All believe in wind.

## V. Into Durango

It's dusty down toward the end of the line.
Raucous, daredevil mountain whitewater,
the aspens trembling in its wake and
strands of snow still clutching peaks,
have given way to dust devils and trailer parks,
lone ponies in bare half-acre lots.
It's hotter far below those Alpine reaches,
where lie misplaced golf courses,
suburban lawns, and the tame, blue man-made ponds
at "The Ranch—Durango's Greenest Acres."
From squalor to nouveau riches in a few clicks
of steel wheels on rails into Durango. I've arrived.
Dusty, I said, and now add: dry.
Why do they need to irrigate the 19th hole,
and the other 18, and each neighbor's garden?
I've been a stream flowing.
I'm not ready to evaporate, not ready to turn to dust.

## Walkabout Rivers

### I. THE COLORADO

#### MILE 0: FOR STARTERS

Let me now visit Earth at its birth.
In Vishnu schist along
Colorado River's bed, twist back
one-point-seven billion years
to this planet's beginning, when the body
of God— if you can believe— created
itself and began twirling in sunlight.

Then let me seek those deep, unsettled
waters of myself, my ancient soul,
so young by Zoroaster granite standards,
down at Grand Canyon's wild, roaring base.
Geologic time places my flesh against
rapid and rock, dampens my fingertips, my lips,
with silty spray: Another époque begins.

## Mile 75.5: SOS

For two days I have been thinking
about the silence of the rocks, their mute looming presence
lit by sun growing toward Solstice fullness,
lit by moon waning at its cycle's end, and lit by stars,
Polaris so clear, bright at turn of night.

For two days I have been wondering
how such ancient rocks might speak to me,
in what language, with what song, and how I should tune
my ears to their key or fix my eyes on their profiles
and shadows.

But now I know you do not listen
to Tapeats Sandstone and calcified Travertine
to learn their hard lessons
in fault line or wind abrasions.
I *feel* their psalms in my broken skin,
seep of blood, deepening bruises,
when Little Colorado River current sweeps
me away to green water pastures—
or into the strong arms of the holy boatmen,
my confluence of buoyant angels.

*for Andy, Chuck and Amy*

## Mile 166: Canyon Colors

Color terror white
and cast it on the river—
am I meant to float?

The bottom of time
is lustrous, polished black schist—
welcome home to Earth.

Seeing blue and red
morning, sky wraps canyon walls—
easily smothered.

Here jade waters flow
designing waves and whirlpools—
first peril, then peace.

Many-pointed truths
emerge from sand and limestone—
night grows gray; I rise.

My wildness is brown—
days of desert sun on my skin
turn me to driftwood.

## MILE 213.5: STRANDED

No shit, there I was
landlocked in Las Vegas,
not a dory in sight,

no boatman with his oars.
I was swept away again—but
in a torrent of yakking tourists

as thunderous as Granite Rapids.
What terror to be tumbled around
in flumes of racing taxi cabs,

not a spume or spray to be seen.
Suddenly, my eardrums burst
from a thousand jangling slot machines.

(Wherefore sweet stream through slot canyons?)
Then, blinded by neon, I saw stars
in my head for there was no starry night.

They whisked me away to safety at last.
The only thing the EMTs heard me say was,
*Send in the bats, please send in the bats.*

## II. The San Juan

### Entering the San Juan below Montezuma Creek

No preliminaries, I simply zip open this river,
unfasten her rustling current to her bare muddied breast
of mute sandstone, hissing silt.
My fingers seek her swirling pulse.
She parts green-trimmed skirts of Earth,
lies down along cottonwoods,
and bids me enter the glistening flow,
to know her naked urgency for gravity.

# Anthropology 101: Beneath No-Name Ruins

Time passes:
Blue herons wade morning river channels;
noon belongs to sky-high ravens on the hunt.
For a San Juan evening? Agile cliff swallows ply
sun's last curve into tomorrow.

Situations change:
This serpentine course we slowly follow,
water singing with silt, the sandstone alcoves
and tiger-washed walls echo waves of
a Pleistocene ocean receding distantly.

Things happen:
Utahan columbines bloom in a flash of white faces,
pearled pink spurs; sprawling cottonwoods submit to monsoon
floods; and only yesterday a people called Anasazi painted
mystifying landscapes of signs as the situation changed upstream,
and that thing called death happened.

*for Kate Thompson*

## Flow Going above Comb Ridge

*I report home to my friend*
*about the constant flow:*

Southeastern Utah's San Juan River dreams a dawn
downstream—olive-brown, brisk, tricky, insistent,
remembering herself surging into the arms
of the Colorado at the pair's forgotten confluence.
I see she hurries to him, both rivers steady as ravens
floating thermals along looming canyon walls.

*I describe for my friend*
*the constant flow:*

Flecks of quartz flash forth from the core
as a crystal dance, what I see
in salmon-tinted layers of Navajo sandstone,
laid down according to the geologic law
of original horizontality.

*I tell my friend*
*of this constant flow:*

Of visitations—
Anasazi ghosts swaying forever
in a shamanic breeze of time,
their slowest gestures incising
the far future into straight facets of rock.

*I report home*
*Earth's constant flow.*

## Shall We Gather at the River?
*with a line from Ann Zwinger*

I am not the first
to have this strong sense
that canyons are not for people—
they're for rivers. And rivers
are here for rocks, to receive
from limestone walls great corrugated slabs
and make of them these billion cobbles.

I am not the first:
Other passing *Homo sapiens sapiens*
who came long before me knew canyons
are not for us. They're for lizards,
mule deer, desert mountain sheep,
green-violet swallows, martins, and bats.
Creatures of the evening primrose,
creatures of the cloudless morning-blue
vault of heaven we are not.

And I am not the first
to take home sand in my shoes,
pebbles in my pockets,
mementos of the San Juan Goosenecks,
testaments to time's endeavors
as I pass through with you this hour,
floating this river's ancient meander
beneath her crumbling canyon towers.

## Approaching 0 Flow CFS

Invincible September stalks summer,
advancing to seal shut the season with frost.

How may I grasp the abundant warm moisture
of the San Juan River where I floated last June?

How may I breathe wisps of nebulosity?
I close my eyes to shut out recollections

of silt swirling midstream and in eddies that
encircled me with glinting bronze waters,

as strands of my hair swept wildly in upcanyon winds
into a nimbus of silver. Now the memory is sepia-tarnished.

And what of the polished limestone oval I purloined
from shore, my smooth souvenir, the one I clasp

in my dry palm as if to recreate the current's embrace?
I hold captive these millions of calcium carbonate molecules,

but they whirl away from my hand, dispersing
the wan halo of San Juan's eons of labor.

Autumn begrudges its glimpses of ephemerality;
evaporation dissipates my confluence with the river.

*Note: CFS is the volume of a river's flow measured in cubic feet per second*

## One Hard Lesson

Cultivating a modest rock garden inside my house,
I scatter stones on shelves and sills
or deposit them in desk and dresser drawers
so I may stumble across them at odd moments.

When I strain for a slim volume on geology,
one by McPhee, a chunk of granite sparkling
with Herkimer diamonds dislodges. Or unrefined
turquoise far from Mexico's Rio Grande is shoved aside

as I wipe dust off the kitchen window ledge.
Smooth, heart-shaped Lockport dolomites line up,
paperweights I have gathered from Lake Ontario's
shoreline fifty feet from my front door.

Fossil-bearing Texas sandstones share a glass bowl
with Alaskan jade and a miscellany of Ordevicians.
Others in a jewelry box are of origins unknown.
Ones I intentionally return to periodically,

when I crave exposed geologic layers
to study depths within myself: my precious Vishnu schist,
a scant handful of chips and bits of that ancient
stone I unearthed near the Colorado River

at the base of the Grand Canyon's inner gorge.
From a worn Ziploc, I release the precious few,
near-black shards on near-white flesh of my palm,
near-timelessness on my curving brief lifeline.

I collect these solid stories of the Earth
to remind me who I am on a Sunday morning,
knowing the destiny of every rock is to become sand.

## Top to Bottom

I follow my complex neo-cortex
along the Grand View canyon rim.
That reasonable and enlightened
animal insists I shall not fall
two thousand feet to my death—
splash in the Colorado River, splat
on the bottom. *Go ahead,
stand on the edge, you won't
slip on Kayenta sand, promise.
Geology is a good thing to witness.
Follow the peregrine's eye.*

But I follow my amygdala, that ancient
and deeply buried limbic creature.
I heed its voice; basic instinct
hisses at me: *Stay, stay away
from the basement rocks, avoid
the Paradox Formation at all costs.
O, big-brained, two-legged woman,
fear is the best thing
in your survivor's handbook.
Follow me like the whip-tailed
lizard; cling to the wall
of red sandstone, safe after all.
Go wild again; live.*

## Marie's Corn Rosary

My mother would have liked
to see this country, its nap of juniper
in the Sangre de Cristo Mountains—
best usage of Jesus's name, no wasted blood
causing bloodshed ever since it spilled,
only the rust-blood of iron ore in stones
sifting into the Rio Grande.

My mother would have liked
to have been an adobe maker,
a gourd tender,
a native woman resisting conquistadors,
a Puebloan matriarch teaching
her children, including me, the peace
to be found in a field of Anasazi beans.

My mother would have liked
to believe in Mary, who was her namesake,
never calling her *Guadalupe* or *Dolores*,
but keeping faith in high desert rain,
praying away the thorned priests of pain:
May monsoons return full of grace
to bathe the Earth, praising maize.

# A Vocabulary of Circular Forms

## At the Ranch above Taos

### I. David Herbert Lawrence

Time is different under the influence
of juniper berries, piñon tang,
and Lobo Mountain frost in September.
On warmer afternoons a man comes
to sit in the blue-green glimmer
of a grand ponderosa a hundred years old,
easily a hundred feet above his head.
He grows small, quieter, like a bark beetle,
and lets the sough of a New Mexico zephyr
ruffle yielding needles as he walks his pencil
across the page and each word becomes a phoenix,
tender as the pine seed from which his shade arose.

## II. Georgia O'Keeffe

Where time is different a painter toils.
*His* tree fills *her* eyes, as does
the ghost of a man perched there
on a bench below, some essence of him
in its branches as she reaches for blue-green,
brushes it, then dabs subtle gray oils
to depict mist rising in the cooler early evening,
washed over in stillness. Each touch shapes
a pool of slender moonlight to render
the impression of impressiveness.
Indelible is her abstraction of his hold
on this place, rooted in vivid passion.


## III. Karla Linn Merrifield

Time is different when I traipse
to Bertie's shrine, his tree now
ninety years taller. I try to see it
through Georgia's bold eyes.
With permission from the keepers,

I tuck three heavy pine cones into my pack—
one for him, one for her, one for me—a trio
for innocence risen from ashes in late evening wind,
for devotion lashing heavy boughs in a thunderstorm,
and for the moon going dark then hastily returning.

In this circle of shadows, we dance
creation until the blue-green dawn.

## Georgia O'K

Details are confusing, she said.
Because I believe in her voluptuous
blue mountain, red sky, and

study in white that could be a rose,
I dispense with my usual lyrical
embellishments to follow her footsteps
in the arid climate, along shallow arroyos,
snipping a few sagebrush leaves,

eliminating everything except
their heady fragrance after evening rains,
their resin on my fingertips.
All that lingers is that tangy essence,
locus where my emphasis comes to rest—

one single inhalation in the high desert hills.
She painted boldly with muscular strokes
in oils, pastels, watercolors, the shades
of new water in all its holy moods,
leaving me to recreate this entire landscape

with one lingering scent for a woman.
I peel away piñons and junipers,
and their sharpness in the freshened air,
so what I create for her is pared down to
"Bared Skin with Sprig of Sage."

# O'Keeffe: "Circling Around Abstraction"

I study her unique vocabulary
of circular forms again today.

First I speak of full moon in full sun.
I speak of red stones alone,
smaller atop larger, two cobbles together
in red dusk. And I speak of
green rivers coiling through
their patient green meanders.

Then I pronounce the word *pelvis*,
pelvis of vibrant visions in a bowl of bone.
I pronounce the blues in blue Western skies
and distant blue desert mountains.
And I pronounce myself conversant
with radiant, round expectancy.

Finally, I recline in purple silence
and listen to oil, watercolor, graphite
whispering to papers Japanese and wove.
I hear brush on canvas.
I whirl 'round, I spiral 'round.
I follow Georgia's sweeping, round touch

and write within her circle
with the circle of the universe.

## From KLM to GO'K: Santa Fe Watercolor Abstraction on Paper: Juniper, Titmouse
*with a line from Georgia O'Keeffe*

Why a tufted titmouse's
gray feathers are charcoaled
in morning shadows

Why he gives the crested impression
of shunning the piñon jay's
indigo allure

Why he ignores me as he swallows
one powdered blue-black orb
of a juniper berry

Why it will one day turn
New Mexico's red hills
rocky dust fragrant green

Why the tree's spiraled limbs
tinged yellow in bold brushstrokes
before my eyes

Whether in the desert's violet
or its orange-hot light on my page
why a single seed passed

by a tiny bird became
my *unexplainable thing
of nature*— in their shades

seeing a new rainbow.

# The Talisman Artifact

This is my hereafter, this woman's bedroom. I am the shell she once caressed each long-fingered morning. Though I am only the bleached carapace of a desert box turtle, my last clutch laid years ago, I am the almost-white creature from the White Place of Georgia O'Keeffe—

(almost as white as these plastered adobe walls and wide white-white window ledges of her hilltop Abiquiu home...almost as white as clouds she set adrift against turquoise skies over blue mesas...almost as white as the jimsonweed blossom, her locoweed in bloom, the sacred datura made bold).

Of all the colors of New Mexican rainbows coalesced in white, she retrieved me from her sandstone heart—she chose me, Bone Mother, the ivory one to curve into her dreams.

## Painting of Sagebrush (Green), Clouds (White), and Raven (Black) on Rice Paper with Wax

Low-ground: Rio Grande, liquid orange at sunset.
High-ground: Sangre de Cristos blood red before dusk.
Mid-ground: the indigo empyrean between.
Earth turns violet on black wings.
The sage Cloudraven of Taos see night's yellow stars
in eyes, obsidian-black,—making blue come
into the artist's micaceous backlit orbs
afire in the blackness of space.

## Land Marking

solitary mesa straining against high prairie skin
breaking free to breathe thin plateau air
shepherding cattle   alpaca herds   sheep folds
dwarfing cottonwood windbreaks   windmills
pioneers from the Santa Fe Trail
sighed relief south of Raton Basin
on these broad green expanses   named
the formation Wagon Mound as if a Conestoga
of brown stone   such a long way from home
to this corner of what was once *viejo México*
east of the *Sangre de Cristos*
despite coyotes   locoweed
storms   drought along the river
its velvet grasses seemed the right land
to settle in   fend off Apaches   await railroads
stay for I-25 to come through
where antelope remain to roam

# The Void

Welcome, no road sign reads
in this region where you lose all time,

all distance, not to mention yourself.
Point your fingers on the paper map,

at all the ninety empty basins and ranges
in Nevada's high desert lands.

With too few fingers, you're mesmerized,
needing more than both hands

to navigate this terrain of faultlines,
how it shrinks humanity, how it favors lizards.

Your GPS reports nothing of this discontinuity
in civilization: outpost country, exile country,

loneliest dust-and-stone country that defies the grid
of your imagination. You forget your original

destination and discover a blank space, that missing part,
the lacuna in your vagabond body, its lost soul.

## A Fragile Defiance
*with a line from Robert McGinty's "A Chaos of Contingencies"*

Bristlecone centuries hold steady
against *the mania of control.*
Millennia of marble, granite, gold,
the silver eons of uncontrollable erosion,
submit to the mind of wind and ice.


*for Roberta Moore*

## It Is You Who Are Essential

I once held a chiseling rock in one hand,
a second hammer rock in the other,
and over the course of brief cool days
in desert's winter etched in a third rock
my maze, tracing the light path of my life.
One thousand years later when I returned,
it was still there, my story: how I met you,
Coyote in the labyrinth of Red Hills,
the tricky, heat-licking Sonoran dreamscape.
Why, you Old Man, you! You're alive
and still tricking in my modern world!

How did you know I would come back?
Retracing my steps up and out of the arroyo,
around and around to your stronghold,
I followed your song: Yips and yowls stir me;
you flaunt wildness, haunting my tame nights.
I shall let you lead me through constellations
of inner space, farther down, deeper into my self.
I shall let your howling teach me for all time
to remember my illuminated hunger.

## Mesa Verde Vision

How in the world did you get here, Mother?
How stirred your ashes from the seabed
of Lake Ontario, spirited them up through

the depths, broke over the waves & breathed
the cool June air again along the shore?
Did you stow away in my Oldsmobile

this journey west with me across prairie
& into the mountains towering?
Or, did you fly as a Western raven flies,

diving towards one exact spot
or gliding on thermals with no sense
of time or destination other than more sky?

Why was it you appeared on my public tour
into Mesa Verde, standing next to Clyde,
the Navajo guide? Why on earth were you sitting

comfortably, legs crossed, winking at him
as if you knew all along what he was going to say
& would have said yourself if you could have?

But, you did, didn't you, Mother?
You appeared in a vision in the cliffs,
where the home fires once burned for Anasazi

to remind me where I came from,
to applaud where I am going. And to let me
know I'll always need you to get there.

## Under the Sleeping Rainbow

In the thunderbird month of July,
like an Aeolian dervish, I come twirling
from redrock rims. As an acrobat

on a katabatic swirl down slope from palisades,
I fly to this valley of desire.
Where a blood river gushes after

another afternoon monsoon, I rush to you.
Like fast wind through
a savage heart eons old, a soul

unafraid of riding gravity, I arrive.
No one else is here to guide us.
No other man, no other woman,

advises us to stay on the trail.
Where on Earth do we go? Anywhere
if we are to wash the wings of bats

with bare hands before eating with coyote,
before we succor swallows,
sate the raven. You and I

lick rain from volcanic cups
in the afterglow of the storm.
Like lost canyon children weaned

by cougars, we run freely among willows.
Perhaps the very same night,
by starlight, we take the names of stones

at the moment of the dark of moon.
You call me Kayenta;
I call you Moenkopi.

We tumble, make the ground tremble
like the lightning earlier this singular day.
We flash; we flood in the way of the wildest.

## The Missing Force at 36° N Latitude, 107° 57' 30" Longitude

With the sun in its summer house,
afternoon winds beat
the sand's message of heat.
Clouds assemble to drum
thunderstorms. But no rains come.

Where snake should swallow lizard,
eagle swallow snake,
time swallowed whole
the golden bird and its people
because no rains came.

The magnitude of their loss
is the magnitude of their epic
ancient civilization brought
asunder by all the erosional
forces you can name, except one.

When no rains came after
solstice morning upon solstice morning
of endless draught, the wind, worse
than any desert wind they ever witnessed,
a life-abrading wind, roared and roared.

And gravity toppled the Anasazi
gods from atop their canyon temples.
Great edifices of sandstone
and great walls of rock and mortar
baked and frozen for eons,

tumbled into ruins—
Chaco without the force
of water,
Chaco becoming a message
of the dust.

## Be Now My Anasazi

I vow never to ensnared by hard places,
as narrow as the path between them proves to be.

I'll use small words like *hot*, *dry*, *stone*,
but not tell you how sere the desert is,

nor say if these walls are sedimentary in nature,
if former gods laid them down in the Jurassic.

We need no scientific terminology for geology.
I would not lead you into highland canyons

without trust in my primitive lexicon.
So I will keep my sentences fleet.

As quick as mountain thundershowers.
Quick as flash floods.

No matter which river, which season,
we will be able to pass through, across.

An alcove in the cliff awaits.
We will begin to paint.

We shall color our love ocher.
We picture it beyond the river narrows.

# Amazons of the Anasazi Follow the Chimney Rock Tour Guide

Note this ceramic, sheep-like vessel,
wavy lines represent fur,
so ethnologists speculate.

> *Only the women*
> *skinned and tanned*
> *their pelts. Only we*
> *shaped their effigies*
> *in the living clay.*

According to certain authorities,
this is a feather-holder, most likely
to hold large turkey quills.

> *Only the women*
> *dipped tips into sacred*
> *ochre ink to write on*
> *bird skins. Only we*
> *were rock artists.*

Although it's still open to interpretation,
scholars believe astronomer-shamans followed
the 18.6-year Lunar Standstill Cycle.

> *Only the women*
> *read celestial calendars,*
> *told when and how*
> *to worship the moon.*
> *Only we kept the stars.*

Archeologists as a whole concur:
The ancients must have been resourceful farmers,
canny hunter-gatherers.

> *Only the women*
> *knelt at metate altars, manos in hand,*
> *and said proper prayers. Only we made*
> *rice flour, corn flour, singing*
> *echo-chants to beans and squash.*

Such clever master masons of prodigious stonework—
212 structures at this site—from great kivas
to little pit houses strewn across the *cuesta*!

> *Only the women*
> *shared the vital secrets*
> *of appropriate architecture;*
> *only we precisely aligned*
> *ramparts with the phallus*
> *now called Chimney Rock*
> *and the breast of Companion Rock—*
> *balanced Earth.*

About the Ancient Puebloans' disappearance,
their migration? Did soil depletion force them away?
Civil war? Enemy attack? Climate change?

*Only the women knew:*
*It was time to go.*
*Only we saw you coming*
*and coming and coming*
*long ago.*

We don't know.

## Araneidae Among the Anasazi

In the days of maize plenty
and squash abundance,
in the land of then-adequate rain
and pliant clay,
my grandmother was a spider.
Each morning she wrote
alphabetmagic;
each evening she erased.
At noon she wove worddreams;
at midnight she unraveled.

During seasons of kiva spells
and adobe smoke,
in rimrocks of Arizona
and alcoved dwellings,
my grandmother was *G. elipsoides*.
By sunlight she drew poemprayers;
by moonshine washed.
Below blue painted epicmyths;
below black she effaced.

For generations her people
thrived on petroglyphs, pictographs
honoring her creations.
But her tribe disappeared
like earthrunes after sandstorms.

Her story crawled slowly
into lonely stone quarters
with me attempting to retrace
all that mystery of art undone.

Grandmother, please spin another line,
cast your web around, around me.

## Stations of the Rock

I.

Crossing the Continental Divide,
I flow toward Pacific shores,
but only so far, only into northeastern Arizona.
I arrive like snowmelt in spring
from the slickrock flanks
of the Chuska Mountains
in a gush toward my destination:
along Chinle Wash through Canyon de Chelly
to the foot of Spider Rock—*Tsé Na'ashjé'i*—
who slows me to within a trickle
of total evaporation, then....

II.

To the Navajo, she of the twin monoliths
is spirit uniting earth and sky,
strong in the union of all things.
I know her as the one with power
to settle me into complete stillness.
Each red blood cell carries
my six senses on breaths of purity.
Her force—the wisdom of how to weave
and what to weave and why—stuns me,
and for an instant I also rise eight hundred feet
above the valley floor where the stream
has run freely for two million years

III.

Like her, I find myself standing tall,
withstanding the tests of time and sand.

# Throb

> *No, a butterfly's waking*
> *dance there, at the spot where light would start*
> *if the heart pumped light instead of blood.*
> —Floyd Skloot

My heart pumps at morning glow
on piñon, on juniper evergreen;
it quickens with silver sage and white datura.

My heart pumps the glossy
raven of the cliffs, lizards
on the noonday rock.

My heart pumps the shining
enchantment of sunset
on red sandstone, red dust.

My heart pumps lightning,
phenomenon of desert evenings.
It skips beats during monsoon thunderstorms.

My heart, racing now, pumps the polished
night waters of Chinle Wash,
all that glitters in Canyon de Chelly.

And then my heart pumps the light
of lunar standstills,
of a supernova.

My heart pumps the Milky Way.

# Lithic Scatter

I wade into the sand wash
the one called Chinle
cool my feet
stand in the shadow
of the cool north
canyon wall
cool my heart
dusty   heated
under the weight of place

I encounter Maria
in red cotton skirt    long sleeves
tending goats    sheep
in coyote-willow shade
after morning's descent
long steep trail    talus-riddled
from rim to floor's flood plain
long return to the top    straight-up
for this mother of eighty-seven years
I blow her a kiss like a maid
gives her fairy godmother
she grins    almost toothless
almost    timeless

So like a maid    I am
supplicant weaver
bowing    bowing
to Spider Rock—
Her Majesty *Tseyi*—

most ancient of us all:
stone bones   singing
my blood warms to a rush
I become in my bones
in my soul   stoned into silence
with no word for the warp of life
how to keep the maid alive
keep from splintering

one kiss   one prayer
I blow behind me
as I ride out
to Where the Mouth Is
if not a girl again
then a poet with
much more to learn
about coming of age
in Canyon de Chelly

# Acknowledgments

My thanks to the publications in which many of these poems or earlier versions of them appeared:

*Adventum:* "Canyon Colors"
*Ahh! Moments:* "Wild Westing" (three excerpts)
*A Little Poetry:* "A Fragile Defiance"
*Avocet, A Journal of Nature Poetry:* "Badlands Sutra"
*Blueline:* "Everything's Talking"
*Boatman's Quarterly Review:* "Mile 75.5 SOS," "Mile 213.5: Stranded," "One Hard Lesson"
*Byline:* "Cody Museum II – Preservation"
*Doorways and Pathways Photography-Poetry Exhibit (RochesterInk Poetry in Fusion Festival 2006); published in The Eleventh Muse:* "At VV74 Fate Bell Archeological Site"
*Elsewhere: A Journal for Literature of Place:* "Rocky Mountain Lows," "Maria's Corn Rosary"
*Hamilton Stone Review:* "Georgia O'K," "Flow Going Above Comb Ridge"
*Hawai'i Pacific Review:* "Amazons of the Anasazi Follow the Chimney Rock Tour Guide"
*Laundry Lines* (Bandini Books): "Grand Canyon Mile 27: Wash Cycles"
*Le Mot Juste 2009:* "Badlands Beauty"
*New Mexico Poetry Review:* "At the Ranch above Taos"
*New Millennium Writings:* "Under the Sleeping Rainbow" (Honorable Mention Award)
*Oregon Literary Review:* "Lithic Scatter" (as part of the essay, "Stanzas from the Stone")
*Poetica:* "Historical Marker, State Route 158"
*Regime:* "Into Durango"
*Remembering Faces:* "O'Keeffe: 'Circling Around Abstraction'"

*River Poems*: "Approaching 0 Flow CFS"
*River Poets Journal*: "Amid the Bighorns"
*Sacred Stones: How the Power of the Earth Can Change Your Life*: "Caution: Women at Work"
*Santa Fe Literary Review*: "Magnitude 5.4"
*SLAB*: "Dancing with Green Bees" (later reprinted in *Crone, Women Coming of Age)*: "Making Beds"
*South Dakota Review*: "Feet of Clay," "Seeing Red in the San Juans' Rainbow"
*Tapestries*: "Parsing Mato Paha"
*The Centrifugal Eye*: "Raven Woman's Artifact, 1862"
*The New Verse News*: "Copters"
*The Prose-Poem Project*: "Summer Morning in Muir's Park," "Talisman Artifact"
*Three Coyotes*: "Rainier Trail Guide"
*Time, & Time Again*: "Mesa Verde Vision"
*Tonopah Review*: "Colorado Mile 0: For Starters," "Great Divides"
*Weber: The Contemporary West*: "Top to Bottom, "High-Altitude Spectrum," "The Missing Force at $36^0$ N Latitude, $107^0$ 57' 30" Longitude;" "From KLM to GO'K: Santa Fe Watercolor Abstraction on Paper: *Juniper, Titmouse*;" recipient of the Dr. Sherwin Howard Award 2012
*Untitled Country Review* – "Entering the San Juan below Montezuma Creek," "Painting of Sagebrush (Green), Clouds (White), And Raven (Black) on Rice Paper with Wax"
*US Workshop*: "$12^0$"
*Yellow Medicine Review*: "Araneidae Among the Anasazi"

This book is dedicated to all those whose friendship and influence helped make it possible, including Andy Hutchinson, Kate Thompson, Chuck and Amy Wales, R. J. Johnson, and Brad Dimock of the dories, and in memoriam to Derald Stewart, Zen boatman. These pages are also a tribute to Nick Bartlett, Georgia Garr, and Nicholas Bartlett of the *Tahoma*. My thanks to all the editors who found merit in the poems and placed them within the pages of their journals; and to fellow writer Laury Egan for her meticulous and graceful editorial assistance, and to Stewart S. Warren for transforming a raw manuscript into an elegant, expressive book.

I am also indebted as always to my beloved husband Roger M. Weir, muse of muses, for his attentiveness in proofreading the many drafts of the poems herein and for holding on to me whenever we crash through the rapids of life. *Gassho*.

# About the Author

**Karla Linn Merrifield** recently received the Dr. Sherwin Howard Award for the best poetry published in *Weber - The Contemporary West* in 2012. A seven-time Pushcart-Prize nominee and National Park Artist-in-Residence, she has had 300+ poems appear in dozens of journals and anthologies. She has eight poetry books to her credit, the newest of which are *The Ice Decides: Poems of Antarctica* (Finishing Line Press) and *Liberty's Vigil, The Occupy Anthology: 99 Poets among the 99%*, which she co-edited. Forthcoming from Salmon Poetry is *Athabaskan Fractal and Other Poems of the Far North.* Her *Godwit: Poems of Canada.* (FootHills) received the 2009 Eiseman Award for Poetry. She is assistant editor and poetry book reviewer for *The Centrifugal Eye* (www.centrifugaleye.com).

Visit her blog, *Vagabond Poet*, at http://karlalinn.blogspot.com. Write her at klmerrifield@yahoo.com, and visit her on Facebook at http://www.facebook.com/karlalinn.merrifield.

www.ingramcontent.com/pod-product-compliance
Lightning Source LLC
Chambersburg PA
CBHW070532100426
42743CB00010B/2047